
70



22 9 22 2 2 2 2 2 2 2 2



and the second s



....

1.022222

i,

0 00



-

- 1

., .,,

.....

1961-1 21 2 221

2 2 2

The state of the s

10 80 10 40 40 40 40

......

.....

.

.....



.

.

1

*

....

COMMAND AND AN ARREST

4 7 477 3545 5 55 5 5 5 5 5 5 5

i and a second



- - -

7 a 5.5

.

155-255-3

1 --

.....

100.00

1 21

AND THE REPORT OF THE PARTY OF

The second secon

and the second s

1 1880 1 0 0 80

.

.....

.....

.....

.....

. . .

. . .

Primary and the second



.....

1

